T0128793

My Roller Coaster Ride with Sallie

An Alzheimer's Story

Judy J. Harritan

authorHOUSE®

AuthorHouse™
1663 Liberty Drive
Bloomington, IN 47403
www.authorhouse.com
Phone: 1-800-839-8640

© 2013 Judy J. Harritan. All rights reserved.

No part of this book may be reproduced, stored in a retrieval system, or transmitted by any means without the written permission of the author.

Published by AuthorHouse   7/23/2013

ISBN: 978-1-4817-7775-9 (sc)
ISBN: 978-1-4817-7776-6 (e)

Library of Congress Control Number: 2013912551

Any people depicted in stock imagery provided by Thinkstock are models, and such images are being used for illustrative purposes only. Certain stock imagery © Thinkstock.

This book is printed on acid-free paper.

Because of the dynamic nature of the Internet, any web addresses or links contained in this book may have changed since publication and may no longer be valid. The views expressed in this work are solely those of the author and do not necessarily reflect the views of the publisher, and the publisher hereby disclaims any responsibility for them.

Preface

My mother, Sallie, suffered from Alzheimer's during the last years of her life. This terrible disease affects more than just the person who has it. Everyone who loves and gives care to this person is also a victim. I have often told people that "if you haven't been there, you don't understand." Of course, this statement is true of many situations, including the sudden and unexpected death of a loved one or death by cancer or another disease. However, Alzheimer's is especially cruel because it results in the death of a loved one before the end of that person's physical life.

Dealing with my mother's Alzheimer's has been very difficult for me. Sharing my mother's story in writing has helped me cope with this disease. I admit that I do not have all of the answers on how to deal with a loved one's Alzheimer's. I just hope that I can help someone else by providing my thoughts and experiences.

I have spent many years dealing with my mother's declining health and her Alzheimer's. It is my hope that I will be spared from this disease as I age and that my family will not suffer my loss until I actually die.

Be sure to read <u>CHAPTER 4</u>: **Notes from Interactions with Sallie**. She was truly a special person. We laughed and had many fun times even after her Alzheimer's began.

Everybody loved Sallie!

In Loving Memory
of
My Mother,
Sallie Todd Jordan

Table of Contents

Chapter 1:

The Beginning of the Ride

*A*s a child, I always had a fascination with the roller coaster. There was something about the anticipation when going up the hill. And then there was the fast fall downward. I always loved the roller coaster, but my ride with Sallie was much different.

Sallie was my mother. I called her by her first name because she eventually came to no longer know who I was and that she was my mother. But she always knew her name was Sallie. Please understand that I was not being disrespectful of her. I just felt that I needed to get to where she was in her own mind. At her death, my mother was in the final stage of Alzheimer's—a disease which may be worse than cancer or death. Alzheimer's may not be worse for the person who has Alzheimer's. I do not know. But I do know how difficult it was for me as a caregiver.

Sallie was married to my daddy Clyde for 57 happy years. I know that Clyde & Sallie were very much in love. Whatever Sallie wanted (within reason), Clyde provided for her. My mother was very spoiled. While they were not rich in money, Clyde and Sallie were certainly rich in the pleasures of life.

Sallie and Clyde

The first time Sallie and Clyde went out together was on a double date with Sallie's sister Eva and Clyde's brother Charlie. However, on this first outing, Sallie was with Charlie and Eva was with Clyde. Apparently, they all realized quickly that was not the best match for any of them because later Clyde married Sallie and Charlie married Eva. Sallie and Clyde married on April 13, 1938. Sallie was 18 and Clyde was 23. They had three children. I was the middle child.

Clyde, Sallie, Sidney, Judy, and Nancy

Sallie was a homemaker her entire life except for a brief job early in the marriage. Whenever anyone would remark that she never worked outside the home, Sallie always reminded all of us that she had worked for three months as a salesperson at a retail store. Sallie was a good homemaker and mother. Nobody cooked better fried chicken than Sallie. Of course, she will best be remembered for her chocolate fudge, coconut cakes, and other sweets.

Clyde was a railroad engineer. After a brief time in the Army and several other jobs, Clyde began his career with the railroad, where he worked for 35 years until he retired in 1979. In the beginning his job as a railroad engineer was on a line between Rocky Mount and Wilmington, North Carolina. This usually resulted in his being in Rocky Mount (where we lived at the time) one day and in Wilmington the next day. Because of this work schedule and his need also to have a place to live near Wilmington, Clyde and Sallie purchased their first beach house at Carolina Beach in 1954. The house was a very small house. It was painted red so we called it the cracker box like the red saltine cracker boxes of that time.

Our family then began to spend our summers at the beach. There was some discussion at one time about moving to the beach permanently, but the decision was made to remain in Rocky Mount during the school year and stay at the beach in the summer. The summers at the beach were great. Who could ask for a better life?

After my younger sister graduated from high school in 1970, Clyde and Sallie moved to the beach full time. Since the beach was now their permanent residence, they purchased a larger house which they had moved next door to the cracker box house. This second house was where they remained until Clyde's death and Sallie's relocation to assisted living.

After Clyde's retirement in 1979, they traveled, played cards, laughed, and enjoyed life. I have numerous pictures of Clyde and Sallie together. In most of the pictures they were touching each other and laughing. Clyde could not keep his hands off

Sallie. You could see the love in their eyes. It was a relationship that anyone would envy.

Clyde and Sallie—always laughing

In 1991 Clyde was diagnosed with prostate cancer. Sallie became his caregiver until his death on November 26, 1995, the Sunday after Thanksgiving. Clyde was 81 and Sallie was 76.

My roller coaster ride with Sallie began when Clyde died. From that point Sallie's life began tumbling down. For the first six months she grieved and did very little else. Then in the summer of 1996 the North Carolina coast experienced two major hurricanes, Bertha and Fran, that made it necessary for Sallie to leave her beach home and go inland during the storms. She spent Bertha in Wilmington and then came to my home for Fran.

Fran was an especially strong and damaging hurricane and flooded the downstairs of my mother's house. My sister Nancy, my husband Don, and I helped Sallie clean up the damage. We also helped Sallie sort through many things that had belonged to Clyde.

And thus began the healing process of the loss of Clyde.

After Hurricane Fran, Sallie began to start living again. She visited her local senior center and made new friends. She even went on a flight and then a cruise in Alaska with two ladies from the center. It was so good to see Sallie active again. She was able to live by herself at the beach for more than 6 years after Clyde died. My sister and I helped her during this time— ordering and sorting her medicine, assisting with her finances, visiting often, taking her for visits with her siblings and with our own families, etc.

But things began to change.

Chapter 2:

Early Signs of Sallie's Alzheimer's

hen I look back, I can see some subtle signs of Sallie's Alzheimer's that I did not fully recognize at the time they occurred.

Perhaps the first sign was how she handled our leaving after a visit. In the past she had always walked us to our car to see us off. However, she began to stay in the house, close the door, and lock it immediately when we left. Not like Sallic at all. She was beginning to change.

There were other signs. When I would call her and asked what she had eaten, her standard response was "bacon and eggs". In retrospect, I am not sure she was eating anything at all.

She would tell me that she took a nap. I think maybe she would gct up, take her medicine, take a nap, and then take her medicine again—not realizing it was the same day and she had already taken the medicine for the day.

Sallie had always loved to read and watch television, but she stopped doing both. She would just sit or lie around and do nothing.

When I would visit Sallie and ask her to go to lunch, she would tell me to go without her. Sallie had always been a little stubborn and wanted to do what SHE wanted to do. Therefore, I knew that insisting that she go to lunch with me would never work. I would "soft" sell the idea. I would tell her that I was really hungry, but I did not want to go to lunch by myself. I would just sit and wait. In a short while, she would go to her room to dress and we would go to lunch.

Sallie also began to think that her neighbor was stealing from her—one of the classic signs of Alzheimer's. Her neighbor was the best. He watched out for her, cut her grass, and was really the only reason she was able to stay at home as long as she did. I really trusted him and I did not think he would steal from her.

Sallie continued to live at home alone until she became ill and had to go into the hospital. When she left the hospital, she was sent to a rehabilitation center where she fell twice, breaking her ankle and her wrist.

While in this facility, Sallie exhibited another example of her Alzheimer's. One month while she was there she called me 71 times and my sister 69 times—all long distance calls. She called me at home during my work hours when she should have realized that I was at work. One day she DID call me at work. She had never called me at work before. Sallie was very unhappy that she had to be away from her home. Maybe she sensed that she would never return there to live.

After her three months in rehabilitation, her doctor decided that it was no longer safe for her to live alone and that she was not capable of managing her affairs on her own because of dementia.

And so the roller coaster ride picked up speed.

Thank goodness Sallie had been wise and prepared for her future before her Alzheimer's began. When Clyde was diagnosed with cancer, he and Sallie prepared their legal documents and their funeral arrangements (including selection of their caskets, purchase of their cemetery plots, etc.). After his death, she visited her attorney and revised her legal documents including naming me as her legal representative in her power of attorney.

When her doctor said that Sallie could no longer live independently, I invoked the power of attorney document at the courthouse and began the search for a new home for Sallie. We had previously looked at some senior facilities together; but Sallie, like most people approaching this stage of life, was convinced that it was not necessary for her. She said she would move into a senior facility when she needed to do so. Of course, she did not realize that she would not be mentally able to make that decision when the time came.

Since I knew that Sallie was not going to be happy anywhere but home, I sought an assisted living facility nearer to me instead of near her home. I was working fulltime and felt I could not adequately care for her if she lived too far away from me.

I will never forget the drive—an extremely long 50 minutes—from the rehabilitation facility to the assisted living facility. I sat in the back seat and my husband Don drove. Sallie was in the front passenger seat. Sallie complained non-stop all the way and we just listened. She asked over and over where we were going. We would tell her and she would respond in a disgusted manner (and with a little profanity). Every once in a while she would say, "Are you listening to me?" and we would respond, "Yes, we're listening". There really was not much we could say because she would not have listened anyway. She was very upset with us for not taking her back to her home.

Why did I not just take her to my house? I did not take her into my home for several reasons (or you may say I have several excuses). The first reason was that I was working fulltime. The second was that I knew that I could not care for her in my home without destroying myself and my marriage. Maybe this was selfish, but I would be no good to her if I did not take care of myself while I cared for her. The third reason was that Sallie had said numerous times that she never wanted to live with any of her children. She knew that would not be in the best interest of anyone. This last reason really helped me cope with the fact that I did not take her into my home.

While I still have some regrets that I did not bring Sallie into my home with me and my husband, I know deep down that it would not have been best for her, for me, nor for my husband. With Sallie in a nearby facility, I was able to visit her often and to manage the care she received. I was also able to work fulltime and continue my normal activities and home life.

While Sallie was in several facilities for rehabilitation, she spent most of her time in three facilities. Let me tell you about the three.

Chapter 3:

Assisted Living, Rehabilitation, and Skilled Nursing Facilities

1st Facility—Assisted Living

Sallie stayed in her first assisted living facility for almost 4 years from September 2002 until July 2006.

The first year was extremely difficult for her and for me. On every visit I had with her, Sallie verbally abused me for "putting her" there. I tried to explain, but she did not understand. She thought that she was fine, could take care of herself, and, as she so often put it, "still had her right mind." Workers at the facility said she had no problems except when I visited. When I asked if I should stop visiting, the facility leaders said I should continue to come to see my mother. My husband Don kept telling me that Sallie did not understand why she had to be there and it was useless for me to try to explain. But I desperately wanted her to understand that the choice to leave her home at the beach was not mine alone and that I was doing the best that I could. I wanted her to be safe.

Sallie's Alzheimer's continued to progress during her stay. In the beginning she was very sociable—visiting with other residents in the sitting area, asking every man to marry her (I think she thought she could go home if she was married), and just acting "normal". Of course, "normal" did not last.

Her Alzheimer's was very obvious on her birthday, May 10, 2003. Sallie really enjoyed the flowers she received. She would see them on the table and ask who sent them. We would open the card and tell her they were from her sister Joyce. Over and over, this scene was repeated and each time Sallie would be surprised. She also received a birthday present. It was wrapped the first time she opened it. However, she repeatedly opened the box and was surprised by the gift each time that she opened it.

After the first year, she remained pleasant most of the time. But she certainly had her bad moments. Having been so spoiled by my daddy, she was accustomed to having her way. If she did not want to do something, it was difficult—sometimes impossible—to get her to change her mind.

One example of this occurred when some of her family planned to visit her. I had asked the facility to be sure that Sallie was out of bed and dressed before the family was scheduled to arrive. To ensure this was done, I went to the facility early the morning of the family's visit only to find Sallie in her pajamas asleep on the couch in the visitation room. Sallie was determined to sleep and stay on the couch.

After I got upset and workers urged Sallie to get up, we FINALLY got her dressed. Situations like this were especially frustrating to me. I was trying so hard to make Sallie appear normal to others, especially Sallie's siblings.

In 2003 Sallie's sister-in-law, Nannie Ree, died and we took Sallie on the three-hour trip to Rocky Mount for the funeral. I had told Sallie numerous times that Nannie Ree had died;

however, as we approached Rocky Mount, Sallie realized where she was. Of course, she did not remember why we were there. When I told her AGAIN that Nannie Ree had died and we were going to the funeral, Sallie exclaimed, "Nannie Ree has died" just like it was the first time that she had heard it. That was typical of many conversations that were repeated over and over to Sallie.

In 2005 Sallie's youngest sister Joyce died unexpectedly. Joyce loved my mother and had spent many, many visits with her from the time Sallie and Clyde were married in 1938 when Joyce was only 6 years old until she died at age 72. This was really an early death for one of Sallie's siblings as most lived into their eighties or greater. Joyce always remembered Sallie at Christmas and on her birthdays. Joyce and Sallie were very close and I believe Joyce thought of her older sister Sallie as a second mother.

We took Sallie to the visitation and Joyce's funeral. Sallie enjoyed visiting with family members, but I do not think she ever realized why we were there. It was so sad that Sallie did not remember Joyce. Alzheimer's had taken Sallie's loving memories of her sister Joyce. On the other hand, maybe it was a good thing that she did not suffer with this loss. She was suffering enough with Alzheimer's.

Although I had been pretty satisfied with Sallie's care at the assisted living facility, things changed dramatically in January 2006. To prevent wandering, Sallie was among those who wore a security bracelet. However, the first of January, she went missing—at night. When I was informed the next day, I was uncomfortable with the explanation that I was given. The first thing the administrator said to me was, "Let me tell you something before someone else does." Since I was my mother's caregiver, the administrator was required to tell me and really should have contacted me the night Mother was missing. Did she tell me the next day only because she thought someone else would tell me? The official report I received from the administrator was not the same as the information I received from some of the facility residents.

I then began to question other aspects of the facility. I felt staff members were not being honest with me. I have always believed that I can deal with the truth, but do not lie to me. I have a difficult time forgetting lies.

After several other problems in the next few months, Sallie wandered off again. This time she left the facility before day, walked two blocks, and was found walking in the highway. An employee of a nearby nursing home picked up Sallie and took her to that nursing home. The assisted living facility called me about 10:00 that morning—I think the delay was to allow the facility to prepare its report and to make sure everyone told the same story. However, that story was inaccurate based on facts that I later discovered.

Because I could no longer trust the facility to take care of my mother and to tell me the truth, I felt that I needed to move her somewhere else. I immediately began my search for another facility. I had been comfortable with where Sallie was living for over 3 years. Now that comfort was gone and I had to find another home for her.

And the roller coaster ride continued.

2nd Facility—Assisted Living

I contacted facilities in my town, but no one would take Sallie because she wandered. I really did not understand why her security bracelet would not be sufficient for them, but I was told that they could not take her.

My next choice was 35 miles from my home. Sallie was accepted in an assisted living facility and remained there for two years. I think she received good care at this facility, especially from the nurse I will call Linda. Linda was certainly a very special and caring person—more details later.

Even though her Alzheimer's was advancing, Sallie was still able to visit with the other residents. Some residents were better mentally than Sallie and some were not. She was able to get around with a walker, bathe and dress herself (with some help), and eat unassisted (or with a little help).

My sister Nancy and I would visit often. In the beginning, Nancy or I would often take Sallie out to lunch, but that became increasingly difficult. After a lunch at a fast food restaurant one day, I decided that I could no longer take her out by myself. It was getting difficult to get her in and out of the car and I could not leave her for a minute in the restaurant. I continued to visit, but we just no longer left the facility.

While this second facility was good, there were some issues. No facility is perfect. However, this one was very responsive to any problems or questions that I had.

One day I got a call about a situation that they were handling. A male resident with dementia slapped Sallie. Since she had trouble finding her room in the past and had actually gone into someone else's room and even lay down on the bed, I asked if that had occurred with this man. No, he had hit her while they were in the hall. Mother had done nothing to provoke him.

Later the administrator told me that the man had a picture of his sisters and one of them looked a lot like Sallie. Since the man had dementia, I thought that it was possible that in his mind he was back in his youth. He may have been playing with "his sister" and meant no harm to Sallie.

The facility moved Sallie to another hall to prevent this problem from occurring again. They made the move quickly and did not wait for me to question what they were going to do. I felt this was very pro-active and was one example of the quality of this facility.

There were other minor problems from time to time, but the staff responded to any issues and seemed to care about my mother's well-being. I felt this was a good facility.

After almost 2 years here, one day I received a call from Nurse Linda. She told me that Sallie needed to go to the doctor so I contacted Sallie's doctor to advise him that I would be bringing her in later that day. I traveled the 35 miles to pick her up.

When I got to the facility, Mother was very weak. I asked Linda if someone could help me get Mother in my car. I told Linda that my husband would meet me at the doctor's office to help me get Mother out of the car. Linda immediately responded,

"No, I'm going with you." Even after I told her that I really did not expect her to travel the 35 miles with me, Linda insisted.

When we reached the doctor's office, Linda was very helpful in responding to his questions. Linda was certainly more aware of Mother's recent activity—or lack of activity. The doctor sent us to the hospital to have Mother admitted. At the hospital Linda was again very helpful. While I completed the necessary paperwork for the hospital, she went with Mother to her room and helped get her in bed. As soon as I got to the room, I told Linda that I would call my husband so he could take her back to her facility. However, she had already called someone to come for her.

I will always remember how caring Nurse Linda was and that she went above and beyond my expectations. That is saying a lot! My husband tells me I expect a lot of people. I expect a lot of myself and therefore I expect a lot of others.

3rd Facility—Skilled Nursing Care

When she entered the hospital at the end of May 2008, Mother had lost a lot of weight, was dehydrated, and was very ill. She was curled in a fetal position (a sign of impending death I have been told). She was tested to determine her ability to swallow. We were told that she had forgotten how to swallow and should not have anything to eat or drink.

That night she asked for water. I gave it to her because I could not deny her request if she was thirsty. It really did not matter to me whether the water went to her lungs or to her stomach. If she asked for water, she would have it.

I did not think Mother would ever leave the hospital alive and I think her doctor felt the same. However, after three days she improved and was moved into her third facility. This time it was a skilled nursing care facility about 15 miles from my home. Mother appeared to be near death and I thought her stay in that facility would be short. Boy, was I wrong. She remained in this facility longer than either of the other two. She was there almost five years.

Sallie was a very strong person. While I thought she was near death, she had other plans. She rebounded, gained weight, and started walking again. Then after a few months, she started having problems with her balance and began to fall regularly. From the beginning of 2008 until late summer, I received probably thirty calls that she had fallen in the hall or was found on the floor in her room. In consultation with her doctor, we decided it was time to confine her to a wheelchair. She was in a chair for over four years.

Initially, Sallie would try to get out of the wheelchair—not realizing that she could no longer walk. After a year or so her efforts to get up became less frequent, but she still tried occasionally. She had fallen so many times—requiring numerous trips to the emergency room. It was difficult for me to see her in the wheelchair, but she was much safer from injury.

I think Sallie received very good care at this facility. Still I felt it was extremely important that I visit often—not every day but several times a week. As I have said before, no place is perfect; however, this facility was above average and responded to my concerns. Everybody seemed to love Sallie there. For this reason, I think she got extra attention. Also, I made many friends who kept me informed about things I needed to know.

My mother had been near death so many times, but she continued to rebound.

In early 2012 Sallie lost 10 lbs. in two months, stopped eating, and was sleeping almost all of the time. I really felt this was the end and I visited more often. It was very stressful to see her in such bad shape.

When I returned home from my visit one night, I told my husband that I did not think I would see my mother alive again. He said I had said that before. Yes, I had, but I REALLY felt this was the time. Mother was 92 years old and really weak. Well, I was wrong again.

And the roller coaster ride continued.

In March Sallie was back. She began eating again, gained weight, and stopped sleeping so much. She continued on an even plateau until later that year when she seemed to change again—sleeping more and eating less. However, Sallie was still up in her wheelchair almost every day. I was glad because I felt she was better in her wheelchair than being in the bed. I did not want to see her bed-ridden if we could avoid it.

The Todd Family
(except for Willie who was killed in World War II)

Front Row (left to right):
    James, Eddie, Sallie, Joyce, Sam, and Rosella
Back Row (left to right):
    J.E., Henry, John, Rosa, Lizzie, and Eva

Sallie was definitely a strong-willed person with strong genetics. Sallie's parents, John and Rosa, had eleven children—six boys and five girls. Sallie was the sixth child and the middle girl. In early 2013, Sallie had four living siblings—a brother who would be 92 in April, a brother who turned 90 in October, a brother who was 88, and a sister who was 85. I thought Sallie might outlive all of them. She had no major health issues (except Alzheimer's) and no stress. She did not know that she had little quality of life.

She still knew four things constantly—her name (first and last), her birthday (day and month), her mother's name, and her father's name. Beyond these four things she varied in what she knew from day to day. She would mention her children by name sometimes, but she did not recognize her children by sight. Sometimes she mentioned other family members. Sometimes she mentioned a person whose name I did not recognize. Whether she ever knew anyone by that name, I do not know.

Sallie had some hallucinations—more in the middle stage of Alzheimer's than in the late stage. Some people think that hallucinating is a bad thing. I do not. When she hallucinated, Sallie talked to people she knew. They apparently responded to her because she would say something to them and then stay quiet as if they were talking back to her. I think these hallucinations were a good thing. In her mind Sallie had friends and family visit her and she was not alone. What could be better for someone who had always enjoyed talking to people?

Sallie

Other Nursing/Rehabilitation Facilities

Sallie resided in two other facilities during her illness.

The first was a rehabilitation facility about 50 miles from my home. After her hospital stay when she first left home, she entered this facility for rehabilitation. We thought at the time that she would be returning to her home, but her doctor decided she could no longer live alone.

This facility seemed to be a good one. Of course, not knowing what to expect, I am not sure that I could accurately rate this facility as to whether the facility was bad, good, or above average. Through the years as Sallie's caregiver, I learned much about what to expect from a facility and its staff, whether good care was being provided, and what to do to ensure good care.

In 2004 Sallie was in a second temporary facility for rehabilitation after a second surgery on the foot she broke in 2002. This facility was about 30 miles from my home.

This rehabilitation facility was not good in my opinion for two reasons. The first reason was the facility did not respond adequately to my requests as a caregiver. Please understand. I was not very demanding. I asked what I considered were reasonable requests from a caregiver—to let me know when the facility scheduled doctor's appointments so I could attend, to keep me informed on any changes needed in Sallie's care, etc.

On one occasion, when I visited the facility to see my mother, I was told that she had gone to a doctor's appointment (about 50 miles away). Even though I had asked in advance to be informed of such appointments, the facility had not done so. My mother's memory was not good and it is possible that I could have helped answer the doctor's questions for her. Obviously, the facility did not think it was important for me to participate in my mother's care. I disagree. After all, I was her daughter and certainly knew her better than anyone at this temporary home could possibly know her.

A second (and much more important) concern I had with this facility concerned moving my mother from her initial room to the Alzheimer's Unit. The Unit was a locked down area with only 8-10 rooms and a dining/sitting area. Sallie definitely declined in that environment. In retrospect, I think she may have been over medicated. She was a different person and never quite got back to her "normal".

During Sallie's stay in this facility, I had several discussions with the facility's administrative staff about my concerns. However, I never really felt they listened to me. Thankfully Sallie's stay in this facility was short-term.

Comments on Facilities in General

Facilities are reviewed and regulated by outside agencies on a regular basis. However, to insure the best care for a loved one, family members must monitor activity in a facility—whether it is a hospital, assisted living, skilled nursing care, or other facility. This is not an easy job to do. Here are my tips. They may not be the best ones, but they are a start for you.

Tips for Insuring Good Care in a Facility

- **Visit often.**
  Every day is not necessary. Once or twice a week may be acceptable.

- **Visit on different days at different times**
  The element of surprise is helpful. If they do not know when you are coming, hopefully the staff will make sure everything is being done properly just in case you show up. I know this is not always the case, but surprise visits do help.

- **Stay in touch with what's going on with your loved one in a facility.**

    Let me give you one example of what I mean:

One day I asked for a list of Sallie's medications. I really did not know what she was taking and just wanted a list. However, after completing a consent form and requesting information for August and September, I received more information than I had really sought. I received a printout of the medications she had received each day from mid-August through mid-September.

When I reviewed the information, I found an interesting list of medications which were supposed to be given PRN ("as needed" basis). She had received one medication seven times in the last two weeks of August and nine times in the first 18 days of September. One particular nurse had given Sallie the medication five times (out of seven) in August and seven times (out of nine) in September. The notation she made was "For Anxiety". Because this raised a big question in my mind as to why it was given routinely by this one nurse, I discussed the report with the nursing home administrator (the director of nursing was out that week).

The main concern I had was Sallie's sleeping. For the previous two months she had slept the majority of the time when I visited her. Because of the report of the medicine Sallie had received, I felt maybe I had an answer for that—the PRN medicine made her sleepy. Based on my observations, "Anxiety" was certainly not a problem for Sallie at this time.

After I expressed my concerns about the medication and a review was conducted by the facility staff, this medication was discontinued. As a result, Sallie began to be more alert than in the previous two months. She would smile, would wink at me, would eat better, and seemed healthier. If I had not requested the list of medications, I wonder how long it would have been before someone realized there was a problem.

While I am sure there are those at the facility who thought I was a lot of trouble, I felt that my questions were important for my mother's well-being. She could not ask questions. Therefore, it was my responsibility to do so. I was Sallie's eyes, ears, and voice.

- **Participate in activities that are provided for family members.**
  Some facilities have events such as open house or special occasion celebrations (Mother's Day, Father's Day, etc.).

Also, a Family Council may exist at the facility. Attend these meetings as they may offer helpful caregiver information from outside sources. For about eighteen months when Sallie lived in the skilled nursing facility, the Family Council offered programs on Alzheimer's, hospice, legal issues, facility staff and their responsibilities, etc. This information was very helpful to me.

- **Get to know the staff** (especially the ones providing the actual care for your loved one) **and their duties**
  Knowing the names and duties of individual staff

members will help when you have questions or encounter problems.

Due to schedule rotations, it is difficult to learn the names and duties of everyone, but it does help. Everyone wants to be important. Calling a person by name and getting to know that person can be a real plus—for that person, for your loved one, and for you.

- **Complain if necessary, but don't sweat the small stuff.**
  This was particularly difficult, especially for me.
  I wanted the best for my mother and I expected
  the best.

I am sure some staff members would tell you that I complained about everything. That is not true. I did suggest changes and I would complain if needed. But remember, my mother had Alzheimer's. I was her eyes, ears, and voice. She could resist and defy some actions by staff, but ultimately it was my responsibility to be sure that she received excellent care.

- **Remember to say "thank you" and "I appreciate what you are doing".**

Chapter 4:

Notes from Interactions with Sallie

*S*allie was always a real character and a pleasure to know. You never knew what she was going to say. Everybody enjoyed spending time with Sallie.

My aunt Joyce (Mother's youngest sister) and my cousin Margaret told me how much they enjoyed visiting my parents after Sallie and Clyde were married. Joyce and Margaret were young girls and enjoyed spending time with Sallie because she played games with them and Sallie always had candy and soft drinks at her house.

After Sallie left home and was in different facilities, she continued to say things that were unexpected and many times were funny. When caring for a person with Alzheimer's, I have learned that you have to enjoy the fun times and the funny (or unexpected) comments that the person makes. There were many such times and comments with Sallie. Let me share some of the more memorable ones.

January 2004

Even early in her Alzheimer's journey, Sallie could disguise the fact that she did not remember information.

In January 2004 Sallie was in the hospital for a second surgery on her ankle. While in the hospital, a female friend came to visit. Sallie and her guest visited for thirty minutes or more and had a very pleasant conversation.

I listened as they talked back and forth and I was glad that Sallie recognized her guest. However, as soon as the woman left, Sallie turned to me and asked, "Who was that?" I had no idea—and neither did the guest—that Sallie did not know who the woman was. Sallie was able to have a polite conversation without ever recognizing the person who visited.

On other occasions when asked a person's name, Sallie's response would be "my honey". She did not know the person's name, but she knew she could get by with "my honey" to identify the person.

In another example of hiding her inability to remember, Sallie would respond to questions with "Don't you know?"

Even with her Alzheimer's, Sallie could pretend that she knew people and could avoid answering questions presented to her. She really had a knack for covering her memory loss.

May 2004

Sallie's first assisted living facility had various events which included family. In May just before Mother's Day, the facility had refreshments for the female residents and their families. I attended and was enjoying the visit when Sallie started talking about her mother. Here's how the conversation went:

Sallie: "Where is Mother? She was here the other day and she promised she would be here today."

I tried to distract her without telling her that her mother had died years before. Since it was raining, I told her, "It's raining outside. It's too nasty for anyone to be out."

She kept insisting that her mother was supposed to be there and continued to question me.

"Is she sick", she asked.

"No, she's not sick," I responded. You have to remember that her mother had been dead for 35 years.

Sallie: "Would you tell me if she was sick?"

Judy: "Yes, I would tell you, but she's not sick." The next question really surprised me.

Sallie: "Has she disowned me?" Of course, I responded "no", but the question made me wonder. Had Sallie made her mother really mad sometime? I did not know of any problems between the two of them. Was there some unresolved issue in Sallie's mind? I will never know.

Sallie continued to ask why her mother was not there. I finally told her that her mother was no longer living, but that she was with her and watching over her.

An agitated Sallie responded, "And I didn't go to the funeral!" I assured her that she did go to the funeral and that we all went.

A few minutes later she asked me if her papa was dead also. Of course, I had to respond that he was also gone.

Questions like these were difficult to answer, especially when I did not know how much Sallie really understood. Of course, her comprehension varied from day to day. I had always been honest with my mother; however, sometimes my honesty may have been a half-truth—not really a lie, but not really the complete truth. Sometimes a half-truth was easier and better for both of us.

2005

I went with Mother for a follow-up visit with her eye doctor. The assistant tested Mother's vision to determine if her eyesight had improved. When asked if she could see better, Mother turned to me and said, "I don't know. Judy, can I see better?" Mother had definitely begun to rely on my help as "her eyes".

2007

Often when I visited Sallie, we would go out for lunch. More than once, she got concerned that her husband Clyde did not know where she was. The conversation would go like this:

Sallie: "I've got to find Clyde. He doesn't know where I am" OR "I've got to go. Clyde is waiting for me."

Judy: "It's just you and me today. Just the girls are having lunch. Clyde is fine. He knows where you are."

We would go back and forth throughout our lunch until Sallie finally remembered. She would ask if Clyde had died, and of course I would tell her yes. These conversations were very difficult for me because I felt I had not been completely honest with her. However, I thought it was better not to tell her Clyde had died until she remembered that he was gone.

Spring 2010

One of my fondest memories of conversations with Sallie occurred in early 2010. I visited my mother and asked her how she was feeling. She responded that she was really tired. When I asked her what she had been doing, I was surprised at her response and the ensuing conversation. Remember that my mother was confined to a wheelchair in a nursing home and had not left the building. However, her last home was at the beach.

Why was she tired? She said, "I've been to the beach."

While I know you should not pressure an Alzheimer's patient for answers, I decided to pursue her line of thought. I asked her, "How did you get there—in the car, on the train, on a bus?"

Sallie said, "In the car."

Judy: "Who did you go with?'

Sallie: "That couple. That man and woman."

Judy: "What are their names?" I could see that she was thinking and trying to remember. Since it appeared to me that she was struggling, I said, "That's okay. It doesn't matter what their names are. What beach did you go to?" Now remember that she had lived at Carolina Beach.

Sallie: "Carolina Beach. But we went farther than that."

Judy: "Did you go to Fort Fisher?" This is an area south of Carolina Beach.

Sallie: "No, we didn't go that far."

Judy: "What did you do?"

Sallie: "You know. We just walked around and talked."

Judy: "Did you go ON the beach?"

Sallie: "It was kind of like sand." I had no idea what that meant to her.

Judy: "Did you go IN the water?"

Sallie: "Yes, but just my feet."

Judy: "Was the water cold?"

Sallie: "No, it was not cold."

Considering how far advanced that Sallie was with Alzheimer's, I was really pleased with this conversation. My mother had not left the building. She had a big day and she was tired. Mother had no idea where she was, but she had "been to the beach." I learned to enjoy the light moments and to get where she was in her mind. Doing so helped me cope with Alzheimer's.

Our Favorite Place
Carolina Beach, North Carolina

2010

On a visit one day by my sister Nancy and me, Mother was not hungry and did not want her lunch. The staff put Sallie down for a nap so Nancy and I left for our lunch. When we returned, the room door was closed and we heard laughter. As I entered, I asked the workers what had Sallie done.

One responded that Sallie said she was hungry when she woke up. The worker had said to Sallie, "Good because we have saved your lunch plate for you."

Sallie then asked, "What are we having for lunch?"

Worker: "If you're hungry, you'll eat anything."

Sallie's response was, "Would you eat a pile of sh--?" And then, the laughter. You never knew what would come out of Sallie's mouth—sometimes nonsense and sometimes remarks that were right on target.

2011

I have read that it is important when death is near to let your loved one go and to tell them it is okay to go. One day Sallie said, "I want to go where my mama is."

I responded, "If you want to go where your mama is, that will be fine. We're okay here and it's okay if you want to go where your mama is."

A few minutes later, Sallie said, "And I want to go where my papa is." I again responded that would be fine and that we were okay here. I waited a few minutes but was curious as to what Sallie was thinking. I then asked her where her mama and papa were.

Sallie responded, "They're out there in the yard."

Where did you think they were? The yard was not where I was thinking they were when she first asked. I told her she could go see them in the yard if she wanted.

Early 2012

I do not know why, but for some reason I began to document Sallie's comments to me when I visited. She said some really unusual things sometimes. I knew I would not remember them if I did not write them down.

One day when I was moving Sallie from the nursing home day room to her room, this was how the conversation went.

Judy: "Let's go to your room so we can visit."

Sallie: "How do I know I can trust you?"

Judy: "You can trust me. My name is Judy."

Sallie: "Judy what?

Judy: "Judy Jordan". Although I am married, I thought it was best to tell her my maiden name.

Sallie: "That's my name."

Judy: "I know. We're kin."

Of course, Sallie had no idea that she was my mother. Her not knowing me was difficult at first, but I became accustomed to it. She did not even know my daddy and they were married over 57 years. That was really sad to me.

Later in the day as we talked, I remarked that I had known Sallie for 60 years. She immediately responded, "I'm not 60 years old." I told her I felt like I had known her all of my life. I was 63 and she was almost 93. After some discussion, Sallie decided she was 57 years old so I remarked that we were about the same age.

Mother and I have always gotten along very well. I have never really argued with my mother. I learned many years ago that I should not argue with her. Now with Alzheimer's, it was even more important. Arguing and disagreeing with her would not help. She was doing the best that she could.

July 2012

As I was leaving after my visit with Sallie, I told her I loved her and I would see her later. Usually when I did this, she would just repeat the "I love you"; but today her response was different. What she said was, "I hope I'll be here." Was she playing with my mind? Who knows? Many times when I left I would wonder if the visit would be my last one with my mother.

July 21, 2012

As I was leaving the nursing home, as always I told Sallie that I loved her. Her response today, "You just lied to me."

I answered, "I didn't lie to you. I have never lied to you."

She responded, "I was just kidding." Then, when I asked her if she loved me, she said, "SURE I do." This was a response that was vintage Sallie—a response that I had heard many, many times from her before and after her Alzheimer's began.

As I said earlier, I guess I have told Mother some half-truths (not really a lie, but not really the complete truth) since she got sick.

September 25, 2012

When Sallie awoke from her afternoon nap, she began talking. She wanted to ask the blessing. I told her to do so if she wanted. She said a short "blessing" or prayer and then talked to God a little—not a prayer, but a direct conversation. Then she told me, "I want to go where God is."

Since I have learned that it is important to let a person go, I responded, "That's fine if that's what you want to do." We had had this conversation numerous times in the past and I always wondered if this would be our last time together.

After visiting Sallie, I told my husband many times that I did not think I would ever see her again. Unlike many other illnesses, Alzheimer's is very unpredictable as to its length. I believe that Alzheimer's had affected my mother for maybe twelve years at this point. She was 93 and had been away from home over ten years.

While she was still physically with us, she was not the mother I knew before Alzheimer's. For me, my mother had been gone a long time. I lost my mother when I could not talk with her and share my life with her. I had grieved her loss and yet she was not gone. There is a term for that type of grief—anticipatory grief.

I knew I would miss Sallie when she was gone, but I already missed my mother.

I visited, loved, and cared for a nice, old lady who did not know who I was. Sometimes she would say she did not know me, ask who I was, or tell me she had never seen me before. I would tell her my name was Judy and that I was her new visitor. I never tried to convince her that I was her daughter. She did not remember.

October 10, 2012

Today Sallie was very talkative. Most of her comments were random and had nothing to do with anything current. Here are some of comments:

"See that man over there. We need to get a search warrant." I don't know where this came from unless someone in the facility said something about a search warrant. Often Sallie repeated words that she had recently heard.

"Nancy keeps that beside her bed." There was nothing in her room that she could have seen that could prompt this statement and I had no idea what the item was.

"Judy, put the baby blanket and all that stuff together." She did not know I was Judy and was not talking to me. Was she thinking about something belonging to one of my sons?

"Nancy, I think we've got everything straight. If you will go back there and pick out what you want." Was Sallie thinking about what my daddy left when he died or what was cleaned out of Sallie's house when she left home?

"Don't you think it's going to look pretty when it's put all around?" Was Sallie working in the yard with her roses?

One comment she made today did make sense. In response to a loud person in the hall, Sallie said, "Don't be so loud." Sometimes she did get in the "real" world, but most of the time she was somewhere else.

Later in my visit, I decided that Sallie must have been planning a party of some kind. Her remarks included:

"Lay all that out in a row."

"Go back there and get a Co-Cola before everybody comes." Co-Cola is short for Coca-Cola. Sallie and Clyde ALWAYS had soft drinks in the house.

"Do you want pecans or peanuts?"

"Nancy, y'all want something to eat? There's some pecans and raw peanuts."

Sallie loved to have company whether in Rocky Mount or Carolina Beach. She really did not do much formal entertaining, but she loved to have a crowd at the house. We had lots of family visit us, especially in the summer at the beach.

Our first house at the beach had three bedrooms, but it was very small. How small? One bedroom had a double bed that had three sides touching the wall. Now, that IS a small room.

The size of the house did not matter. It was not unusual to have as many as six or seven (in addition to our family of five) visit us at the beach. The beach house may have been small, but we had many fun-filled summers and Sallie enjoyed having guests.

November 25, 2012

At this stage of her Alzheimer's many times when she responded, Sallie would just repeat what had been said to her. At the end of my evening visit with Sallie, I told her that I loved her. She replied, "I love you more than you'll ever know." This comment was totally unexpected.

I responded, "I love you more than YOU'LL ever know. You've been such a good mother."

Sallie replied, "I hope I've been a good mother."

It felt like we were actually having a conversation and that Sallie was not just repeating what had been said to her. I do not know if she knew what she was saying, but it certainly did sound good to me.

November 28, 2012

When I arrived at the nursing home, I spoke to Sallie and asked her how she was feeling. She told me she was tired so I asked her what she had been doing. Her response, "Working in the yard." Since it was fall and leaves were everywhere, I asked her if she had finished raking the leaves. She responded, "No, not quite." Sallie had always enjoyed working in the yard. Apparently that had not changed even though she was confined to the nursing home. She still "worked in the yard" in her mind.

Later the CNA (Certified Nursing Assistant) got Sallie down for her afternoon nap. Since the CNA would soon end her shift, she said to Sallie, "Goodbye, Miss Sallie".

Sallie responded, "I'm not gone yet." The CNA and I were surprised but amused by Sallie's response. As she left the room, the CNA changed her goodbye and told Sallie that she would see her later.

Even in the late stage of Alzheimer's, Sallie still said things that surprised me, but sometimes she was right on target with her comment. Then again, she would say something completely "off the wall". Who knows where she was in her mind? It was a mystery that would never be solved.

December 28, 2012

I had believed for a long time that my mother could read my mind.

My husband, son, and I were planning to go on a cruise, but I had not told Sallie that we were going. I did not tell her because I was afraid that she might understand and then be upset that I was leaving or that she was not going with us.

I visited my mother two days before we were to leave. The next day I was planning to finish my packing. While my mother often talked about going (nowhere in particular—just going), she never mentioned packing. Well—that day she did. Of course, that was one of the things I had on my mind that day, but I never discussed it.

I told you she could read my mind. I believe there is a special bond between a mother and a child that enables one to think the same thing the other is thinking. I know this is true of a husband and wife who have been married a long time. My husband and I are good examples of that.

January 22, 2013

When I arrived at the nursing home today, Sallie's first comment to me was, "You are a good mother to me." I have no idea what prompted that comment. Did she think I was her mother? Was it a follow-up to our conversation in late November? Who knows.

Also, today as I was getting ready to leave, I told Sallie that I had to go. She asked why and I told her I had to check on my husband. She responded, "Don't rush off." A comment she had made many times before her Alzheimer's.

After I told her I was not rushing off and that I loved her, she replied that she loved me and then said something about happy. I asked her what made her really happy. She said, "You make me happy." What a bright spot that was for my day with Sallie!

February 21, 2013

This morning started as most visits usually begin in this stage of my mother's Alzheimer's—she slept some, was awake some but had her eyes closed, and was mostly quiet. Usually she became very lethargic after I fed her lunch. However, today after lunch she became very talkative. When she became talkative, I tried to question her softly just to see where she might be in her mind.

Today's conversations (and I mean conversations plural because the topics were certainly not all the same):

Judy: "I love you. Do you love me?

Sallie: "You know I do." I always took note when she responded with something other than a repetition of what I said. To me, this signified that she was thinking and not just copying my comment.

Sallie: "I want to be alone when I go upstairs." Today she has said several times, "let me go." Where was she planning to go? Was she getting ready to die? The next few comments certainly made me wonder.

Sallie: "Please let me go without you."

Judy: "Where are you going?"

Sallie: "Going with my grandmother."

After a brief pause, Sallie said, "Let me go where they've gone to sleep."

After another pause,

Sallie: "Eva, let me go with you." (Eva was Sallie's sister who died in 1991.)

Judy: "Where is Eva?"

Sallie: "Y'all won't let me go where Eva is."

Judy: "You can go where Eva is. We're all fine here."

Sallie: "I want to go when no one else is around."

A few minutes later,

Sallie: "Give me one of them for Mother and Papa when I get home." We rested a little and then I tried a different topic.

Judy: "Do you love Clyde?" (Sallie was married to Clyde for 57 years.)

Sallie: "I hope so."

Judy: "Does he love you?

Sallie: "Of course, he does."

Judy: "What do you like best about Clyde?"

Sallie: "Eggs"

Judy: "Eggs? Why?"

Sallie: "Cause they're good to eat." In the middle of our conversation, Sallie's thoughts had changed to food.

Without any questions from me, Sallie said, "You can eat at home anytime you want to. It'll never make you sick." I tried to get answers from Sallie about her favorite foods, but I could not understand her response.

A little later, Sallie again began to discuss being let go.

Sallie: "I want them to turn me loose."

Judy: "Okay. Where do you want to go?"

Sallie: "Wherever I want to." Even at this stage of Alzheimer's, Sallie's independence was still evident.

Judy: "You can go wherever you want. That's fine."

Sallic: "Please let me sit in there with them."

After Sallie was put down for her afternoon nap, it was time for me to go home.

Judy: "I've got to go. I'll see you later."

Sallie: "How much later?"

Judy: "I've got some errands. I'll see you soon. I love you."

Sallie: "That's what counts."

With all this discussion (much of it started by Sallie) in just a short while, it was hard to believe that Sallie's Alzheimer's was so advanced. Apparently, she did have some lucid moments today. I really believe that she did know what she was saying sometimes. Alzheimer's has been an enigma for me.

March 1, 2013

Today when she was put in bed for her afternoon nap, Sallie was very restless. It seemed she just could not get comfortable. It was unusual for her.

I went home around 3:00. I really did not think much more about Sallie's restlessness until that night when I learned that Sallie's brother Eddie had died shortly after 5:00 p.m. Eddie was 91 years old.

Did Sallie sense that he was dying? Was that the reason for her restlessness? I do not know, but it certainly made me wonder.

I did know that Sallie was still in contact with her deceased siblings at least in her mind because she had conversations with them. Hallucinations? Maybe—maybe not. We will never know.

March 7, 2013

I was beginning to wonder about Sallie. I had read that many people get better before they die.

Today she seemed "in touch" with the things I said to her. Lately she had been answering my questions with appropriate responses. I knew she was not getting better but was she getting ready for the end? I did not know. Time would tell.

Alzheimer's is a difficult disease because of the unknown duration. With many other physical problems, a doctor can give you an estimated time remaining. Not so with Alzheimer's. The disease could last a very brief time or a very, very long time—maybe as long as 20 years. Sallie had definitely been affected for 11 years, but she probably was in the early stage of Alzheimer's two or three years before she left home. She was almost 94 years old, but I thought she might live to be 100. She had no pain, no stress, and no life-threatening physical problems. It was sad that she could not be mentally alert to enjoy her longevity.

March 11, 2013

When I walked into Sallie's room, I was surprised to find her sitting in her wheelchair with her head up. It had become normal for her to sit with her head resting on her chest—sometimes she was asleep, but many times she was just sitting with her eyes closed. Today she was alert. Those days had become very infrequent for Sallie.

Last week I told Sallie that I saw Sam (Sallie's brother) on Tuesday.

Judy: "I saw Sam and he said he's coming to see you."

Sallie: "I bet he won't."

Before my visit today, Sam called me so I told Sallie.

Judy: "I talked to Sam this morning and he said he's coming to see you."

Sallie: "I'll be here." I guess today she was more optimistic about seeing him again.

I had seen Sam last week at Eddie's funeral. Maybe I should have told Sallie that Eddie died, but I did not think she would understand. If she did, it might upset her and she would not remember later that he died (if she remembered him at all).

Later this morning, Sallie asked me for new information—a new question. This was the first time she did not know her name.

Sallie: "Tell me who I am"

Judy: "Your name is Sallie Jordan."

Sallie: "We have the same name."

For a long time I had been able to rely on Sallie's knowing four things—her name (first & last), her birthday ("the tenth of May"), her mother's name (Rosa), and her father's name (John). Was Alzheimer's taking those few things from her, too?

A short time later and without any comments from me, Sallie said, "One more year ought to be enough." What could she have been thinking? Was she predicting her longevity?

Sallie continued to make conversation the remainder of the day. Some of the things she said made sense—some did not.

While many times I could not understand her remarks, she was still talking. Sallie was still using complete sentences most of the time. And, it did seem that lately she was better at responding to questions with intelligent answers.

March 19, 2013

Every time I leave I always tell Sallie that I'll see her later. I don't indicate that it may be tomorrow or the next day because that seems to upset her sometimes. "Later" seems to be a lot easier for her and for me. I also tell her that I love her. Usually she responds that she loves me. Today our conversation when like this:

Judy: "I'll see you later. I love you."

Sallie: "Okay."

Judy: "Do you love me?" I always needed that confirmation even though I knew I was loved.

Sallie: "You know I do. Do you love me like I love you?"

Judy: "Of course, I do."

Sallie: "I love Sallie."

Judy: "I do, too. Do you love Judy?"

Sallie: "I don't know Judy."

Judy: "She's your daughter."

Sallie: "I don't know her."

I do not know why I continued to set myself up for disappointment. I guess I was just hoping that she would remember me. It was rare that she did. If she did know Judy, she did not recognize me as Judy. I guess she was looking for a young girl.

One day Sallie was talking about a little girl. When I asked her if the girl was Judy, Sallie responded, "No, Judy is older than that."

I asked her, "How old is Judy?"

Sallie's response: "14". I am certainly not "14", but it was good that someone remembered me at that age.

March 22, 2013

For the past three or four weeks it seemed that Sallie was responding in our conversations in a more normal manner. She answered and asked questions like a person who did not have Alzheimer's. I knew she was not getting better, but was she getting ready (or trying to get me ready) for the end? Here were some comments from today's visit.

Judy: "Good morning. How are you?

Sallie: "What time is it?" She has not asked or been concerned about time in many years. Why today does she care what time it is?

Judy: "10:15"

Sallie: "I'm going to take a nap." Usually she just fell asleep without any mention of taking a nap.

Later in the morning, I kissed Sallie on her forehead.

Sallie: "That's mighty sweet." I thought that was a very thoughtful comment for her to express.

Judy: "I try to be sweet, but I'm not all of the time."

Sallie: "Me, too."

Sallie slept (or at least had her eyes closed and her head down) in her wheelchair until lunch. Even though she kept her eyes closed the entire meal, she did eat some of her lunch.

After lunch, she became more alert. This was really unusual (although it has happened several times lately). Usually she slept immediately after eating.

Without any prior conversation from me, Sallie surprised me with the next few comments from her.

Sallie: **"I'll** tell you one thing." This was a phrase I had heard many times from my mother before she had Alzheimer's.

Judy: "What's that?"

Sallie: "You will miss me."

Judy: "Yes, I will miss you. Where are you going?"

Sallie: "I'm not going to tell you." This was vintage Sallie also—sounded just like old times.

A short time later,

Sallie: "You're not going to like me."

Judy: "I like you."

Sallie: "What do you like?"

Judy: "You're sweet and you're fun."

Later,

Judy: "What else do you want to tell me today?"

Sallie: "I think a lot of you."

Judy: "You do?"

Sallie: "You know I do."

Today Sallie could not tell me her name nor her parents' names. However, she did tell me her birthday ("the tenth of May"). She also seemed to know Clyde (her husband of 57 years) and responded that he was "my honey".

But today was a very special day that I spent with my mother.

Saturday, March 30, 2013

When I arrived at the nursing home, Sallie was sitting up in her wheelchair. She was sitting with her head up and was alert.

Judy: "How are you?"

Sallie: "Tired."

Judy: "What have you been doing?"

Sallie: "Walking from room to room." Sallie was confined to her wheelchair and could not move it so I knew she had been sitting in her room—not roaming the hall.

Judy: "Why have you been doing that?"

Sallie: "The girls came and wanted some help."

Later in the morning, Sallie said, "I wish I could help. Let me help." I guess she was wanting to be needed.

A short time later, Sallie had a grimace on her face so I asked her, "Are you feeling okay?"

Sallie: "No, not really."

Judy: "What's wrong?"

Sallie: "Got a bad headache." A long time ago I had instructed the nurses to give Sallie something if she said she was in pain. We could not know whether she was in pain. If she thought she was, a little medication would not hurt. The nurse gave her something and Sallie seemed to be more comfortable.

Sallie: "I thought Judy would be here in a little bit and she can help." I wish she had known that I WAS there to help.

Having your mother not recognize you was difficult, but it was something that I knew was important for me to accept.

A few minutes later, Sallie began talking, talking, talking, and wanting to help.

Sallie: "Let me go and help them. I want to go. Let me go."

She began to raise her voice and became very, very agitated.

Sallie: "I want to go. Let me go. Lizzie, come and help me. Let me lie down. Lizzie, come and help me. Eva and Lizzie, come and help me. Let me go, Lizzie."

I went for the nurse because Sallie was so upset and appeared to be in pain. The nurse and assistant got Sallie in bed and took her blood pressure which was a little above normal, but okay. Sallie settled down and took a nap. During her nap she jumped a couple of times like she was falling and talked some while she "slept".

Later that evening Sallie had a slight temperature.

Sunday, March 31, 2013

She was somewhat better on Sunday morning. The nurse checked with the doctor and they decided to run some tests. The result was a urinary tract infection (UTI) so antibiotics were begun.

The remainder of the day everything seemed pretty normal for Sallie. We did keep her in bed all day because of the UTI. She slept peacefully most of the day with very little conversation.

Monday, April 1, 2013

I did not visit Sallie on Monday. I did not hear anything from the nursing home and I thought her UTI was under control.

Tuesday, April 2, 2013

Tuesday morning I got a phone call from the nurse to let me know that Sallie was sick. As normal, the staff had gotten Sallie up into her wheelchair. Sallie was fed and she ate all of her breakfast. However, she then threw up everything.

I got to the nursing home about 1:00 p.m. and learned that Sallie had thrown up a couple of times and was having diarrhea. Of course, everyone kept telling me there was a stomach virus going around and that I should wash my hands often so I would not get sick.

When I arrived, Sallie was asleep and slept until about 3:00 p.m. When she woke up, she began to talk—but not to me. She talked to three of her siblings (Lizzie, Eva, and Eddie) who had died. Eddie died very recently—March 1—and Sallie had not been told. She had talked to Eva for years and had begun talking to Lizzie a number of months ago, but she had not mentioned Eddie until today. With short breaks between comments, here was how her conversations went:

"Help me. Help me, Eva. I'm slipping. Don't go down there."

"Come and fix this for me."

"Eddie, come and help me."

"Please let me go. Eva, let me go."

"Let me get up. Please let me get up. I can't rest like that."

"Eva, let me go back there."

"Will y'all help me in?"

"Please let me go." Then some mumbles that I could not understand.

"Eva. Eva, will you listen to me?"

Off and on all afternoon, Sallie moaned and complained once or twice that her stomach was hurting.

"I think I'm going to have to get some rest."

"Can you show me how to open this door right here?"

"Come and help me please." I asked her what did she need, but she did not respond to me.

"Eva, please help me. I can't do it by myself."

"Eva, I can't do nothing. I'm just crazy."

"I'm not well. My body wants to go to sleep and it just won't go to sleep."

About 7:40 p.m., Sallie said, "Eva, I don't believe I can stand this for much more."

"Get me off the bed. Please let me go."

I stayed with her until about 8:00 p.m. I waited so I could talk with the night nurse to be sure she was aware of Sallie's problems that day and to ask the nurse to call me if she needed me.

As I was getting ready to leave, I told Sallie, "I love you."

Sallie responded, "love you."

I went home thinking Sallie had a UTI and a stomach virus.

Wednesday, April 3, 2013

Approximately 2:30 a.m. I received a call from the nurse. Sallie had thrown up blood. The nurse "could not get any O2" and she heard a "death rattle". I told her that I would be there as soon as I could get dressed and drive to the nursing home.

I arrived a little before 3:00 a.m. and knew the situation was not good. Sallie had her eyes partially open and was breathing with her mouth open.

Usually she slept on her left side and she kept her arms crossed on her chest and her fists clenched. This morning she was lying on her back with her right arm to her side.

I picked up her right hand and gently opened her fingers. I had not been able to open her hands in a very long time. I knew that the fight was gone from her.

I sat beside her, holding her hand, and talking to her. I heard the "death rattle" a couple of times, but other than that Sallie remained silent. Her breathing became slower and slower. About 3:50 a.m. she stopped. Her death was very peaceful. She did not struggle. She was ready to go home.

Having that last hour with my mother was very special for me. I had anticipated my mother's death many times over the past eleven years, but she had really gone down fast at the end—much faster than I had expected. She was up in her wheelchair on Tuesday morning and she was gone before day on Wednesday. Even though she was not aware of it, she had suffered a long time from Alzheimer's. But her death occurred quickly. I was so glad that she did not have to be bedridden for a long time. Sallie was too feisty for that.

At 3:52 a.m. the roller coaster ride was over. And like most roller coaster rides, the end was sudden.

Chapter 5:

Pros and Cons of the Roller Coaster Ride with Sallie

PRO

- During Sallie's Alzheimer's journey, I have met and bonded with many special people (her doctor, nurses, CNAs, facility staff, other family members, and extra-special people—other facility residents).

- I have never felt that I had any patience. Alzheimer's has forced me to develop my patience.

- I have had more one-on-one time with my mother than I ever had before.

- Learning to accept someone as she is without trying to change her has been a successful challenge for me. I knew that I could not improve my mother's mind and that I had to adjust myself to get where she was in her mind.

- I have learned how really special my mother was and always had been. Everybody loved her.

CON

- I became a mother to my mother. This was so unnatural and difficult to accept.

- Having your mother forget her husband—a man she dearly loved and was married to for 57 years—was difficult. And, of course, she also forgot her children and grandchildren. She never really knew her great-grandchildren.

- The stress of the ride certainly affected my health. About nine months after my mother left home and I began my responsibility for her well-being, I had a seizure. I will take medication for the rest of my life to prevent another seizure.

- The stress of not knowing what will happen day-to-day was enormous for me. I did finally get to the point where I did not have any expectations of my mother when I visited. If she was alert, we talked. If she slept, I just sat with her.

- I tried (and I think I succeeded most of the time) to be an advocate for my mother. I felt I was her eyes, her ears, and her voice. Trying to ensure proper care for my mother, I felt badly sometimes when I had to report unsatisfactory performance by staff at a facility. However, I do believe that it was important to visit Mother often (and on different days and at different times) and to be seen so staff would provide better care for her. They knew that I was coming; they just did not know when. AND they knew that I expected the best care for my mother.

• When I visited the nursing home to see my mother, I often visited with other residents as well. Many of the ones I visited died. I know death is inevitable, but it still does not make it any easier for those of us who see it.

• I have always been a planner. Therefore, Alzheimer's was very difficult for me. Alzheimer's does not allow much planning for the future—mainly because there is no way to know how long the future is. My mother almost died so many times and then rebounded. And thus the roller coaster ride continued for almost 11 years.

Chapter 6:

Thoughts and Tips from an Alzheimer's Caregiver

Thoughts

- I dream some very vivid (although unreal) dreams. Do these strange thoughts stay in my memory? If I should develop Alzheimer's, will I talk about these things? Will everyone think I am crazy and not just the victim of Alzheimer's?

- When a male does not visit his family member with Alzheimer's, why does everyone make excuses for him? Numerous times I have been told, "It's too hard for him to visit." Does that make it okay?

It was difficult for me to visit and see my mother deteriorate right before my eyes. She did not know her husband of 57 years when I mentioned his name. She did not recognize me. She had to be fed, clothed, and transferred in and out of bed. Sometimes she was alert, but most of the time she was "off in another world".

Why do people think it is easier for a female than a male to cope with and care for a loved one who has Alzheimer's?

• Is it necessary or recommended that you visit your loved one EVERY day he or she is in assisted living or nursing home?

I do not think it is. If you are comfortable with the care your loved one is receiving, it should not be necessary to visit every day. In the initial time in a new facility, it may be good, but later I did not feel I should go every day. My mother did not know me and did not know whether I had been or not. I could go into her room and she would seem surprised to see me, but she would not know me. If I went down the hall and came back, I would get the same reaction from her. Therefore, I doubt it made a difference to her whether I visited every day or not.

Going to visit every day takes a toll on the caregiver. Because of my health, my doctor told me not to visit every day. Visiting was very stressful. I had always felt that I would not be any good for my mother if I did not take care of myself. Maybe you think that is selfish, but I know my limitations.

Visiting every day may destroy the caregiver—physically and mentally. And then who would take care of your loved one. Every day is not necessary.

- Hallucinations are not necessarily a bad thing for a person with Alzheimer's. For a while my mother hallucinated on a regular basis. I could be on her left side and she would talk to someone on her right. She would talk, remain silent for a short while, and then talk again. Apparently, whoever she saw was talking back to her.

  I feel these hallucinations were a real positive. My mother was not alone when I left. In her mind, she had people visiting her all the time.

- I have been told many times by many different people that often a person gets better before he or she dies. Whether it is actually true or not, I do not know. I do not think my mother was better physically near the end of her life.

  However, I do know that my mother's communication improved before she died. She made comments that made complete sense and that were not suggested to her. Just look at the comments she made during the last month (March 1-April 3, 2013) of her life.

Tips

- **Encourage your loved one to prepare legal documents** (will, power of attorney, healthcare decisions, etc.) **before Alzheimer's or other dementia occurs**
Also, prepare YOUR documents and make known your own wishes while you are able.

- **Attend an Alzheimer's support group** (if one is available)

- **Attend Alzheimer's workshops for caregivers**
Whether you are a full-time or part-time caregiver, workshops WILL help you.

- **Talk with other Alzheimer's caregivers**
As I have said, "you don't understand if you haven't been there" so talk to people who have been there.

- **Join Alzheimer's caregiver support websites** that offer facts, suggestions, stories from caregivers, answers to your concerns, etc.

- **Keep a diary**
Sometimes it helps "to write a book" like this one.
It may never be read, but it will give you a way to express your thoughts and feelings.

- **Enjoy the moments of happiness with your loved one**.

- **Get in the mindset of your loved one** (or at least try)
  This will help you understand where he/she is at that particular moment and you can enjoy the past. It may be last week, ten years ago, or before you were born.

- **Learn to repeat without correcting your loved one.**
  I know that it is much easier to say, "I just told you" or "I've already answered that question." However, many times a person with Alzheimer's does not remember. It may frustrate you to repeat, but it would probably frustrate your loved one much more if you tried to convince her that you had already told her.

  Also, correcting a person with Alzheimer's is a futile effort. Correcting or disagreeing will not work. It is much better to accept whatever is being said and change the subject. Right or wrong really does not matter. The person with Alzheimer's probably will not remember the discussion.

- **Take a vacation**

  It is difficult to leave your loved one in a facility while you take a vacation, but it is important for you to have some time away from Alzheimer's. You will provide better care for your loved one if you take a break.

- **BE HAPPY,**

  LAUGH,

  and

  ENJOY THE ROLLER COASTER RIDE!

The following poem by an unknown author helped me and may help you stay focused during the roller coaster ride known as Alzheimer's.

Do Not Ask Me To Remember

Do not ask me to remember.
Don't try to make me understand.
Let me rest and know you're with me.
Kiss my cheek and hold my hand.

I'm confused beyond your concept.
I am sad and sick and lost.
All I know is that I need you
To be with me at all cost.

Do not lose your patience with me.
Do not scold or curse or cry.
I can't help the way I'm acting.
Can't be different 'though I try.

Just remember that I need you.
That the best of me is gone.
Please don't fail to stand beside me.
Love me 'till my life is done.

-Author Unknown

Epilogue

Sallie Todd Jordan

May 10, 1919 – April 3, 2013

allie Todd Jordan, age 93, died on April 3, 2013, at Lake Waccamaw, NC, after suffering from dementia for a number of years.

After 17 years apart, Sallie rejoins her husband of 57 years, Clyde Jordan. Theirs was a match made in heaven and Sallie has missed Clyde dearly since his death. She can now be at peace and spend eternity with the love of her life.

Sallie was born on May 10, 1919, to John Edward Todd and Rosa Matthews Todd. She was the 6th child of 11. In addition to her parents, she was preceded in death by her brothers, Henry, James, Willie, and Eddie Todd and her sisters, Lizzie Todd Mann, Eva Todd Jordan, and Joyce Todd Arnold.

Sallie and Clyde lived in Rocky Mount while spending their summers at Carolina Beach. In 1970 they moved to the beach year-round. Sallie loved Clyde, her family, bingo, chocolate candy, and ice cream. She was fun to be around and she will always be remembered for being a good sport. Everybody loved Sallie. Her life changed when she developed dementia, but she was still a favorite of those who took care of her. The family expresses a special thank-you to the people who loved and cared for Sallie during her final years of life.

Sallie is survived by three children, Sid Jordan, Jr. of Wilmington, Judy Jordan Harritan and husband Don of Whiteville, and Nancy L. Jordan of Garner; four grandsons, Sidney Jordan III of Arkansas, Rick Hufham of Knightdale, Vance Harritan and wife Michelle of Huntersville, and Mark Harritan of Whiteville; 2 great-granddaughters and 4 great-grandsons. She is also survived by 2 brothers, J.E. Todd and wife Frances of Bradenton, Florida, and Sam Todd of Sanford; a sister, Rosella Todd Harrington and husband Johnnie of Willow Spring; a sister-in-law, Doris Todd of Elm City; and a brother-in-law, Bill Arnold of Sanford. Sallie also leaves behind numerous loving nieces and nephews.

Visitation was held at Andrews Valley Chapel, South College Road, Wilmington, from 11:00 a.m. until noon on Saturday, April 6, 2013 followed by a graveside service at 12:30 p.m. at Greenlawn Memorial Park, 1311 Shipyard Blvd., Wilmington.

In lieu of flowers, the family requests that donations be made to Carolina Beach Presbyterian Church, 1209 North Lake Park Boulevard, Carolina Beach, NC 28428; to Alzheimer's North Carolina, Inc, 1305 Navaho Dr. Suite 101, Raleigh, NC 27609; or to a charity of one's choice.

Acknowledgements

Thank you to my sister Nancy and all of the other people who cared for and visited my mother, especially during the final years of her life.

I want to give a special thank you to my husband Don for his patience during my mother's illness and during the completion of this book.

Judy J. Harritan

About the Author

A native North Carolinian, Judy J. Harritan lives with her husband Don in Whiteville in Southeastern North Carolina. She is the mother of two sons and has a daughter-in-law and three grandchildren. Judy retired from a career in banking. In addition to spending time with her family, her hobbies include youth baseball, crafts, and participation in craft festivals. Judy also is an active community volunteer.

Judy's mother Sallie suffered from Alzheimer's for many years. Judy wrote this book to share her experiences as Sallie's caregiver in an effort to help others cope with a loved one's Alzheimer's and to help them enjoy the ride.